MESSY PRAYER

Text copyright © Jane Leadbetter 2015
The author asserts the moral right to be identified as the author of this work

Published by
The Bible Reading Fellowship
15 The Chambers, Vineyard
Abingdon OX14 3FE
United Kingdom
Tel: +44 (0)1865 319700
Email: enquiries@brf.org.uk
Website: www.brf.org.uk
BRF is a Registered Charity

ISBN 978 0 85746 379 1

First published 2015
10 9 8 7 6 5 4 3 2 1 0
All rights reserved

Acknowledgements
Unless otherwise stated, scripture quotations taken from The Holy Bible, New
International Version (Anglicised edition) copyright © 1979, 1984, 2011 by Biblica.
Used by permission of Hodder & Stoughton Publishers, an Hachette UK company.
All rights reserved. 'NIV' is a registered trademark of Biblica. UK trademark number
1448790.

Extracts from *Common Worship: Services and Prayers for the Church of England.* © The
Archbishops' Council 2000.

Cover photo: boy with prayer tree © Ian Leadbetter; girl painting prayer © Ben Mizen

Every effort has been made to trace and contact copyright owners for material used
in this resource. We apologise for any inadvertent omissions or errors, and would
ask those concerned to contact us so that full acknowledgement can be made in the
future.

A catalogue record for this book is available from the British Library

Printed and bound by CPI Group (UK) Ltd, Croydon CR0 4YY

MESSY PRAYER

DEVELOPING THE PRAYER LIFE
OF YOUR MESSY CHURCH

JANE LEADBETTER

PHOTOCOPYING PERMISSION

The right to photocopy material in *Messy Prayer* is granted for the pages that contain the photocopying clause: 'Reproduced with permission from *Messy Prayer* by Jane Leadbetter (Messy Church, 2015) www.messychurch.org.uk'. The right to photocopy material is not granted for anyone other than the original purchaser without written permission from BRF.

Templates are also available to download: please visit www.messychurch.org.uk/9780857463791.

CONTENTS

CONTENTS

INTRODUCTION

'Hands together, eyes closed. Let us pray.'

How many of you remember the first time you were invited to pray? How old were you? Where were you? Who were you with? Were you being instructed, prayed for, or responding with 'Amen'?

Picture this: a six-year-old girl moved house to another area in Derbyshire along with her parents and younger sister. Her mother took her to the local church Sunday school one afternoon. She had not yet had time to make friends, she didn't have any wider family close by, and she didn't know anyone in the Sunday school. At the end of the session, she was invited to listen, along with other children, to a prayer being read from a prayer book held by a Sunday school teacher, and then to respond with 'Amen'.

That young child was me. I can still picture the face of the Sunday school teacher and the large book in her hands. Unfortunately I cannot remember her name. But she wanted me to agree to what she was saying to Jesus on our behalf. I remember thinking at the time, 'How odd! Why is someone I only met today speaking to someone I have never met, on my behalf? Will I ever find out who this Jesus is? When will I meet him? Will he be coming to this Sunday school? Will I be able to talk to him myself when he does?'

Of course, I had no idea that Jesus already knew me. I had no idea that I actually had a best friend there with me on that first day in Sunday school. I had no idea that that best friend would be there for me in the good times, the ordinary times and the worst times. I had no idea that when I grew up I would become a Sunday school teacher and encourage children to say 'Amen' at the end of prayers.

Times have changed. Yes, you did read it right: the Sunday school I first attended was held in the afternoon. I am that old! There are very few UK Sunday schools held during the afternoon now. The Sunday school movement has changed hugely and we need to pray for its future.

I have very happy memories of the various Sunday schools and Junior Churches I attended. I can still picture the Sunday school cupboards, smell their woody mustiness and count the pencil crayons in old food tin tubs. Those crayons always needed sharpening. I can remember the box of story Bibles and the prayer books with curly corners and loose spines, their aged appearance indicating years of being held by children searching for their favourite pages. If you're like me, you may still have some of these books about the house or passed down through the family. You may also have Messy Church cupboards just like this. These days the cupboards are probably made of metal, full of glitter and googly eyes instead of erasers and hymn books, but those old cupboards were suitable for their time.

As the years move on, we adjust to changes and embrace different learning styles, resources, group names, group leader names, venues, times of the week to meet, numbers in attendance and leadership support. But something has never changed. Something has never been locked away in a cupboard from one week to the next. Something is out there right now, and it is powerful and amazing—prayer.

We cannot halt prayer in any of its forms. It is yours, mine and everyone's, for any time. We can pick it up and share it, write it or shout it, whisper it or think it, touch it or hear it, sing it or say it, create it or borrow it, sign it or imagine it. Even those who are incarcerated because of their Christian convictions can silently pray. Someone is always listening: 'Then you will call on me and come and pray to me, and I will listen to you,' says the Lord in Jeremiah 29:12.

An ex-colleague once shared a story with me, which I shall never forget. A very young child went to visit her granny. Granny lived on the ground floor of a sheltered housing complex with a central communal garden. It was a newly planted garden. There were borders of green-leafed shrubs, small grassy areas and a pattern of shingle paths encircling some rose bush islands. In the centre of all this was a large, pink-flowering Queen Elizabeth hybrid rose bush. On the day the child went to visit, it was the only bush in the whole garden that was beginning to bloom. It had one huge pink flower, and the beauty of that flower shone across the garden.

The young child went out into the garden to play. At first she ran around the shingle paths as fast as she could. As Granny watched from her kitchen window, she could see her granddaughter sitting on the lawns, picking the daisies, throwing them up to the sky, then watching them fall to the ground. Then Granny saw the young girl suddenly stop and stare at the beautiful pink rose bush in the distance. It was only a momentary pause in her otherwise speedy exploration of the garden (a garden that the grandmother was very fond of), but Granny sensed an unexpected change in her granddaughter's behaviour.

As the little girl raised herself to her feet and began to walk towards the bush, Granny darted for the kitchen door. As the child gained speed on her journey towards the central bush, so did Granny increase the length of her strides, and as the little girl reached the bush and took the full bloom in her hands, Granny reached out to protect the flower from being plucked from its stem—only to hear the little girl say, 'Well done, God!'

INTRODUCTION

Assumptions—we've all made some. Are we assuming that the Messy Church families we love and care for are praying? Are they praying every day or just when we invite them to do so? Is there a pattern of prayer in their lives? What about the Messy Church teams? Do we assume that they have a praying habit? Or are they waiting for someone to help them along? When do people pray? How can we encourage all ages to pray? And the biggest question of all: why should we pray?

God loves us and cares deeply about us, and he calls us into a relationship with him. Even more than that, he wants us to have a deep and long-lasting relationship with him—a friendship. For healthy friendships to develop, you need to communicate frequently, build trust, and share your concerns and joys. Prayer is a way we can communicate with God. We are commanded to pray ('Pray continually,' says Paul in 1 Thessalonians 5:17), and we must respond.

This book will explore some engaging ways of praying as individuals, as teams, as families and as gathered congregations. It is a challenge, but the Messy Church network is the best sharing network I have ever belonged to. God seems to be blessing what we share and we rejoice when we hear about prayer being answered.

We will look at the fun ways of praying, as well as the quiet, respectful ideas. We will look at including prayer in the craft and activity times, creating prayer spaces and quiet rooms, preparing prayer activities for the celebration time, and praying for teams and all-age congregations. We will encourage the use of imagination and look at ways of becoming reflective.

We all love practical tips and lists of ideas, and you probably have your own. You may have found a children's prayer that an adult engaged with, or an adult piece of music that brought a response from a baby. You may have tried a prayer idea that didn't work very well and another that worked so well, you use it often. We need to encourage each other to keep trying different ideas, to encourage all ages to pray and to pray often and in faith.

Our Messy congregations may be already praying, but, if we need to introduce them to prayer, let's make it an enjoyable and worthwhile experience. And let's not make any assumptions. We can be risky and bold for God. We can create channels of prayerful chatter between our Messy Church families and God. God is so amazing that he can hear all of our Messy chatter, all at the same time. That must sound very messy!

I pray that we stay humble in our Messy prayers, because our attitude is important. Can we encourage our prayers to come often and naturally, rather than from a sense of duty? Are our Messy friendships supporting each other's spirituality and growing deeper with love and respect?

For prayer is nothing else than being on terms of friendship with God.
ST TERESA OF AVILA

THE SPIRITUALITY OF MESSY CHURCH

MARTYN PAYNE

Martyn Payne is BRF's Messy Church team member with responsibility for gathering information about Messy Churches and reflecting on the movement.

You can't get much more down to earth than a big splat of paint on the floor, a tangled web of glue on your fingers or a handful of glitter caught in your hair. But maybe you can't get much more spiritual than this, either?

Making a mess is in the DNA of Messy Church and it is this full-blooded engagement with material things that can also make it a truly incarnational experience. Getting creative in imitation of our Creator brings together all that we are and all that we can be—both messily human and potentially divine.

One of the unhelpful inheritances of some Christian traditions is a separation between the secular and the sacred. No wonder onlookers to the life of faith caricature Christians as being 'so heavenly-minded that they are of no earthly use'! But the truth is that only when we are full of heaven can we make a difference here on earth. Jesus came to unite things in heaven and on earth in a glorious togetherness that rejoices in the paint as well as the piety.

In essence, this is the spirituality of Messy Church. The crafts and activities, the lively interactive celebrations, the creative times of prayer and the enjoyment of tasty meals together are all rooted in the everyday, because it is here that we can meet with God and most powerfully reveal him to the world. As Christians, we sit with Christ in the heavenly places but also with our feet placed firmly on the ground and our hands stuck into the mess and miracles of this marvellous world.

Messy spirituality is a spirituality of the everyday and the concrete. It celebrates the sacredness of ordinary things that can speak to us about God, whether it is splattered paint, a huge junk model or a time-consuming take-home craft— all of which, in themselves, point to God as creator and to his delight in creating. Jesus used ordinary things to speak about the kingdom—seeds, coins, ears of corn and lumps of yeast—and this is what Messy Church is imitating.

It's not just the material things of Messy Church that re-connect us to our innate spirituality, though. Messy spirituality also lies in our encounters with other people. After creating all the beauty and wonders of this world, God crowned his work by making human beings who were to reflect his image. When we put the first description of creation in Genesis 1 alongside its parallel in chapter 2, we realise that it is in community that God finds the best expression of Godself, because God says it is not good for humans to be alone. The mysterious truth of God's own internal community as Father, Son and Holy Spirit is reflected in our shared representation of his character, and so it follows that the best expression of our spirituality—our wholeness in Christ—is found when people come together.

Messy spirituality is a spirituality of the other. It is about rediscovering church as community, where we meet God in each other's differences and discover more about God together, not from a course in a book but from lives that rub up messily against each other. Once again, some strands of Christian tradition have not always been helpful in understanding this. Our spirituality has too often been viewed as an individual, spiritual journey—just me and God working it out together. Mature spirituality is forged in community, as alongside each other we both discover more of God and display more of God to the world.

Celebrating this community spirituality is a distinctive feature of Messy Church. By offering space and time to develop true friendships with each other, we experience a shared communality that reflects God's heart. Journeys of faith should begin together, not in isolation, and those journeys of faith need to be rooted in the everyday world of the objects we work with. It is this mutuality and concreteness that is so attractive about Messy Church and so affirming to people, who are made for each other and made to be creative.

This understanding of messy spirituality can also help to bring a bigger dimension to the concept of prayer. Messy prayer is not an other-worldly, exclusively personal experience of God that involves a retreat from everyday life; instead, it is earthed in material things and the meeting with others. The physical experience of hanging prayer requests on a tree, lighting candles or drawing in sand is also a shared experience in Messy Church, as we gather together around a prayer space or reflective corner and encounter God together. We need each other on a faith journey into the grace and love of God and we need the things of this world to be parables that will signpost the way.

We are God's image not in isolation but in friendship and creativity, and we reveal God to others through our relationships and our remaking of this world. Messy Church offers a home where this can happen. It provides physical things to work with as well as real people to meet, so that together we learn more of who we are meant to be and who God is. We often forget that when Paul addresses Christians in his letters, he is not passing on advice and ideas for individuals to absorb in private. Rather, his words are for the whole church to hear and respond to in its new togetherness. The word 'you' that he uses in his exhortations is plural, because we *together* are God's temple, his hands and feet, his light and a home for his Spirit. Our spirituality could thus be defined as 'our spirits, along with the spirits of others with whom we are in friendship, reaching out to God's Spirit, who, in his turn, reaches out to us'.

Messy Church is offering us a new way, not just of doing church but of doing spirituality and prayer. It puts the conversation back into conversion and the community back into communion. It celebrates our interdependence rather than nurturing our independence, as spiritual beings made in the likeness of God. The paint splat on the floor and the chatter at the tables are exactly where God is to be found— and not just for the children, but for the adults too, so that together they may become aware of the God who loves them, calls them and makes them whole.

There are all sorts of aids to spirituality, of course—practices that nourish our spiritual life, such as prayer, silence, liturgy, scripture, routines, pilgrimage, music, poetry and so on—but the distinctive feature of Messy spirituality is that it is not so easily defined. It is blurred, confused and… messy! This speaks to the spirituality of the Western world today. Life has become very messy in all sorts of ways, and a messy spirituality that connects to the everyday, that is simple and flexible, that connects people easily and quietly with each other and with God in unwordy ways, is just what we need. This is why Messy Church is now a movement with such a significant voice: the paint splat on the floor and the buzz of conversation at the tables offer us a spirituality for our time.

GETTING STARTED

The BRF Messy Church team thanks God every day for all of his blessings on this all-age ministry. We are constantly amazed at how God is working in our communities through Messy Churches all over the world. There are stories on the Messy Church website that blow us away! There are churches working together for the first time and really enjoying it. There are Messy Churches reaching children and adults who have never been to church before. We read about the Messy Churches that are set up in unusual venues to try to connect with communities, such as working men's clubs, pubs and leisure centres. There are churches with Sunday morning congregations of 15, who can serve a meal to a Messy congregation of 100 on a Saturday afternoon. How can we forget about the Bristol church that was due for closure until they started a Messy Church, which proved so popular that they were appointed a part-time minister?

There are too many stories to share here, but none of these successes 'just happen'. They have been steeped in prayer and hope from the very beginning. Well-established Messy Churches are probably still praying for the same things as they did when they first started—for families to attend, for team members to cope with the numbers attending and have enough time to build friendships, for there to be enough food to go round, and so on. But even if the prayers are the same, day after day, year after year, God listens just the same. He doesn't switch off just because he has heard it all before.

It could be that your Messy Church core team instigates prayer. These people may be the ones—passionate, fired up and inspired by God—who first caught the vision for starting a Messy Church. There are lots of you around! God gave you the nudge to become missional in your community. Core teams work together in different ways, so maybe they pray in different ways, too. We hear about core teams who have grown into Bible study groups. As they explore the monthly theme, they open the Bible and discuss what they feel God is saying to them.

I have to admit that at one core team planning meeting for my own Messy Church (L19), we all arrived feeling very tired after a busy day, with no resources or ideas between us. We gratefully accepted the hot drinks and cake and then sat staring at each other for inspiration. One member prayed for everyone on the team, for the day of work just past, and then invited God to be present among us. We found ourselves reading as many Bible versions of our chosen story as were available, and we eventually came up with so many ideas between us that we had too many. We felt energised and creative. God had picked us up, shaken life back into us and given us the best resource of all—the Bible. Prayer had prompted the outcome, and we will never forget it.

The monthly planning meeting times can be very prayerful. At some Messy Churches, planning meetings take place immediately after a Messy Church session. The team members have eaten together and then they review the session and plan the next one. It seems to work well for some teams. They can pray about the previous session and include prayer for the coming session. While events remain fresh in their memories, they pray for the new families who attended, the families who were expected but didn't come, the positive things that happened over the previous two hours, and the things they need help with.

Not everyone can give so much time in one hit, though, so separate planning sessions work best for others. Some Messy Church coordinators invest their time in regular communications. Emails fly off to the team and Facebook posts prompt and help to share ideas. Prayers via email are quite common, it would seem, perhaps inviting teams to offer prayers in advance of a session, which can then be prayed on the day of the session—say, 20 minutes before the Messy Church begins. Follow-up prayers are then emailed between monthly sessions. Some Messy Churches are twinned, praying for each other during sessions as well as at the planning meetings.

If you have a prayer circle for your Messy team before the session, it can be an odd situation for new team members. Not everyone is comfortable praying aloud and sharing their thoughts. Perhaps you could incorporate a news time, asking the team to share news with one another, which you then offer up to God for a blessing. You could invite the team to write their prayers during the meal time with the Messy congregation. (I will talk about this again later.)

The one regular prayer that the core team can offer to God, at each planning meeting, is the prayer for the families who come to Messy Church and the families who have not yet entered your Messy Church. God knows who they are. The family and community prayer checklist could look like this.

- Pray for the relationships between family members. Pray for the parents, siblings and wider members of the family.

- Pray for the children at school during the week and the challenges in the workplace for the adults. Pray for encouragement and safe environments for all.

- Pray about the influences around the families—on TV, the internet, computer games and magazines.

- Pray for the growth of faith in the families. How can Messy Church contribute to the lives of people of all ages, and how will God touch their lives through the Messy activities?

- Pray that each family will receive a sense of belonging to Messy Church. Pray that each person will feel God's presence each day.

PRAYER IDEAS FOR THE ACTIVITY TIME

When all ages are together, some great conversations can take place. Don't assume that families regularly sit down together, sharing meals and talking. Of course it does happen, but we can help to create a space to allow meaningful conversation to happen.

NEWSPAPER HIGHLIGHTS

Place some newspapers on a table, along with highlighter pens. Which headlines or reports concern you the most? Highlight the words to bring them to God in prayer.

FOIL CROSSES

Talk about your mother, father or other special person. Remember special times that you have shared together. Use small and large pieces of aluminium foil to scrunch, tear or fold a cross shape. Hold it in the palm of your hand and remember that Jesus had special times with God, his Father, when he went off to pray to him.

PRAYER CUBE

This activity can be adapted for most themes but, to develop intergenerational conversations, take a blank template (see page 124) and draw or write on the cube faces all the times of the day, month or year when you feel closest to God. Then cut out the template outline and fold and secure the tabs to form a cube. Thank God for these special times and pray for future ones.

WORLD PRAYERS

These prayers can be personal, corporate or informative. Use a large world play mat or globe and talk about places where there is suffering in the world. Highlight the areas with sticky notes or make small models of people from play dough or clay. Place items of rubbish on areas of sea and forests, and talk about the need to look after the world.

FLOATING PRAYERS

Use bowls of shallow water or paddling pools to float prayers. Write your prayers on pieces of paper folded to make flowers or boats, or use floating candles. You could make scourer sponge boats with straw masts and write your prayer on a paper flag attached to the mast.

LAMINATE PRAYERS

Dust off your laminating machine and use the pouches for written prayers, along with decorations such as sequins, coloured pieces of cellophane, tissue paper and so on. Laminate, then cut into shapes and join them together with ribbon. Hang the shapes in a window or on a wall, or use them as bookmarks.

CHENILLE STICKS

One of the most versatile craft items that can be used for prayer is a chenille stick, which can be bent and twisted. Take beads, or cereals, savoury snacks or sweets that have holes in them, and thread them on to a stick. Form heart shapes to show God's love for us, people shapes for prayers about our families, star shapes for Christmas prayers, and so on.

FORGIVENESS PRAYERS

People of all ages love bubbles. Make your own mixture (see the recipe on page 122). Think about something that needs God's forgiveness, blow a bubble and watch it float away. When it pops, imagine the prayer being released to God.

You can purchase specialist paper that will dissolve in water (search for 'magic dissolving paper' on the internet). Write something on the paper that you want God to forgive you for, place it in a bowl of water and watch it dissolve.

Similarly, you can find 'magic flash paper' on the internet. If you write a forgiveness prayer on this paper and set it alight (in a metal bucket or tray, for safety), it will quickly disappear, with no ash left behind—definitely a 'wow' factor.

Bring a bit of fizz to forgiveness prayers by thinking about people we need to forgive, even though they may be hurting us. We do feel hurt and angry at times. Pop an effervescent vitamin tablet into some water and watch what happens. As the bubbles float away from the tablets, imagine that they are passing the hurt over to God.

ICY PRAYER

God listens to every prayer. He listens because he loves us so much: God 'sticks' with us.

Place ice cubes on a tray and cut some lengths of string. Try to pick up an ice cube by placing the string over or around it. Do not touch the ice cube with your hands. The trick is to soak the string in water first. Then place the string over the ice cube and sprinkle some salt over it. Wait a little while and then lift the ice cube by pulling on the string.

GLOOP PRAYER

God's loving touch changes people's lives. Add water to cornflour and stir into a paste. When the mixture settles, it becomes firm, but if you stir it around, it becomes fluid again. Pray for God to change the lives of suffering people.

TEARDROP PRAYER

What upsets God? Cut out teardrop shapes from old OHP acetates, and write prayers on the shapes with a permanent marker. Place the teardrop on a cross-shaped template. How do we feel about God's worries and concerns?

HIDDEN PRAYER

Using a white wax crayon or a household candle, write a prayer on white paper. The prayer will be invisible. Invite someone else to reveal it by brushing over the paper with water-based paint. God knows our thoughts and prayers even before they are revealed on paper. Nothing is hidden from God.

PLAYCHUTE PRAYERS

Playchutes are often associated with children's work but they are enjoyed by all generations and I would encourage you to try playchute activities in your Messy Church sessions. Start with a warm-up, with everyone holding the edge of the playchute at waist height and lifting it up high on the count of three. If the chute does not rise very high, ask everyone to take half a step towards the centre of the circle. This will help.

PLAYCHUTE PRAISE

Simply lift the playchute high as you shout the refrain.

For the fun and games at Messy Church,
Jesus, we thank you!

For the stories and activities at Messy Church,
Jesus, we thank you!

For our families and friends,
Jesus, we thank you!

For the new friends we have made,
Jesus, we thank you!

[Invite everyone to make their own prayer suggestions.]
Amen

Shout 'Amen' out loud and spin the playchute by running round in a circle, at speed, all holding the chute tight to keep it taut.

PLAYCHUTE TENT PRAYER

Hold the playchute and lift it high. Everyone takes one big step forward, pulling the playchute over their heads and down behind them, so that they are eventually sitting on the edge of it. (This will take a few practices.) When everyone is inside the playchute tent, explain that you are going to whisper some sentences and everyone can whisper the refrain each time:

Dear God,
When we are worried and don't know what to do,
Help us to listen to your voice.

When we are frightened and scared,
Help us to listen to your voice.

When we are angry and want to fight back,
Help us to listen to your voice.

When we are busy and haven't time to stop,
Help us to listen to your voice. Amen

PLAYCHUTE THANK-YOU PRAYER

Invite everyone to hold the edge of the playchute and give each person one of the following words to remember: happy, sad, loud, quiet. Each time the playchute is lifted high, call out a prayer that ends with one of the words (for example, 'Jesus, thank you for being our friend when we are... happy'). The people remembering that word have to run under the playchute and through to the other side.

You can sometimes call out more than one word at a time.

PRAYER TRAILS

People of all ages love a trail. Print out a prayer on pieces of paper, including around six or seven sentences, with some missing words. Stick photos or pictures of the missing words around the Messy Church building. Send people off to find the pictures and fill in the words.

For example:

> **Thank you, God, for...**
> **My _ _ m _ _ _ who I _ _ v _ very much.**
> **I pray for my s _ _ _ _ l and w _ _ kplace,**
> **my nan who is in h _ _ _ _ _ _ _,**
> **and my mum who is s _ _,**
> **Help me to be good and make my mum**
> **h _ _ _ _. Amen**

PRAYER IDEAS FOR THE ACTIVITY TIME

For this example, you will need pictures of a family, a red heart, school, workplace, hospital, and sad and happy faces.

CREATING A
PRAYER SPACE

How can we invite our Messy congregations to engage in prayer activities when our space is limited? Prayer spaces can be created in loud bustling rooms and quiet annexe rooms.

At L19: Messy Church in Liverpool, we have an annexe room in the church hall building. We did not make use of the room for the first two years of our Messy adventure, though, as we felt that the team members would rather be in the main room, enjoying the whole atmosphere of Messy Church, than isolated in a room on the side, looking after the activities there. As our average monthly attendance grew to 180, we had to rethink our use of space, and then something happened one November when we had a Messy fireworks session on the theme of 'Jesus is the light of the world'.

After the outdoor fireworks display, I was challenged by some parents who had children with special needs. We had called our session 'Messy Fireworks' on the flyers but we had not advertised the fact that actual fireworks would be set off. Some children had apparently been very distressed by the sudden noises and bright lights, and the parents had not had time to prepare their children for the event. Well, we were mortified! How could we be of help to these families in the future? We asked if they had any advice for us in planning our future programmes.

This was the time when we developed our annexe room into a quiet room. Initially we created a chill-out space for the families who had advised us, but we have discovered how much we all need such a space. Purchasing and borrowing Christmas lights, lava lamps, cushions, blankets, beanbags and CDs of peaceful music was one of the easiest and most unexpected pleasures in our Messy journey so far. We have enjoyed prayer candles in trays of sand, torch shadow prayers, bubbles, floating prayers on water, prayer trails and prayer trees, sometimes linking activities from the hall to the annexe room too.

Creating prayer spaces in busy halls and churches during activity times can be challenging, but we can pray in a variety of ways. God is so amazing he can always hear us. We can enjoy creating a prayer tent or corner or table, for instance. Set out your regular prayer space with a cross made in a previous activity time, easy-to-read instructions and simple activities. All ages love being invited into a 'special' space. If you explain that you have created the space just for them, then it will work.

CREATING A PRAYER SPACE

Keep it simple. Make a prayer tree from large branches or twigs, supported in a bucket or container of sand and stones. I once hung a prayer leaf on a special prayer tree that someone had lovingly painted gold. Or you can purchase wooden prayer trees, such as the Messy Church tree available at www.inf.co.uk.

Borrow a small tent and attract all ages inside with a simple prayer activity, such as using a finger to write 'sorry' in a tray sprinkled with a light layer of dry sand. When you shake the tray from side to side, the word disappears—a sign that God has forgiven you.

Create prayer spaces using music to draw people to the activity, or collect used headphones so that people can sit in a busy room, yet listen to peaceful music in the middle of the noise. Reflective printed pictures on the theme of the month can be displayed nearby or placed in a folder to browse.

EXAMPLES OF THEMED PRAYER SPACES

I love prayer spaces, because you can set them up anywhere —on tables, on the floor, balancing on chairs, in boxes, in cafés, in schools or in parks.

One particularly successful prayer space I visited was a rainforest tent. The theme of the session was 'exploring how we can look after God's world'. A gazebo was covered in green and brown strips of crêpe paper and fabric, hanging from the canopy to the floor. Outside the tent were sheets of information about endangered species and maps of the world. On a table were animal and bird shapes on which people could write prayers. Music and recorded sounds from a rainforest were playing in the background and, after pinning our prayers to a hanging piece of rainforest, we were invited to make a simple endangered parrot that could be balanced on a finger.

Another idea would be to provide small pieces of fish-shaped paper, pens, an explanation of how the disciples felt when Jesus told them to 'fish for people', and instructions about writing a prayer asking God to help each of us to be disciples of God. Perhaps the fish prayers could then be taken to another activity space and placed on to a sea collage or blue wool weaving loom or in a small paddling pool. The fish could be hooked on to a piece of netting or a blue towel or fabric sheet.

The two themes on the following pages were used at 'Messy Quiet Prayers' sessions during the Hand in Hand Children's and Family Ministry Conference in Eastbourne, in 2013 and 2015. The first theme, 'You are special to God', was created for those who work for God in their churches. The session was set up in a bistro area on tiny tables, for just 30 minutes. It was so popular that we had to push people out at the end, before the next seminar began. The second theme, 'God loves you', was appropriate for Valentine's Day, and families from the community were invited to join in. This time, a much larger room was available to us and we could spread the activities out on larger tables.

Stand-alone instructions for each activity can be printed on paper and slotted into perspex A4 or A5 menu holders. You can then step back and invite people to participate, with music playing in the background if possible.

THEME: YOU ARE SPECIAL TO GOD

John 3:16

For God so loved the world that he gave his one and only Son, that whoever believes in him shall not perish but have eternal life.

You will need: assorted beads; cross foam beads; chenille sticks or beading cord (all available from www.bakerross.co.uk)

Make a bracelet or key fob to wear, to remind you how much God loves and cares for you.

St Augustine of Hippo

God loves each of us as if there were only one of us.

You will need: a large heart-shaped piece of paper; pens

Look at the space within the giant heart shape. In a space, write the name of someone who still needs to know that God loves them. How will you let them know?

Job 34:19

[God] shows no partiality to princes and does not favour the rich over the poor, for they are all the work of his hands.

You will need: flower shapes pre-cut from paper (see template on page 125); pencil crayons; bowls of water.

Each one of us is special to God. Colour the paper flower petals and write your name in the middle. Fold the petals over each other in the centre and crease well. Place on the water and watch your name being revealed to God. God created you!

Song of Songs 2:4

Let him lead me to the banquet hall, and let his banner over me be love.

You will need: pieces of A5 paper; pre-cut people shapes; white wax crayons or candles; paint colourwash; paintbrushes

Choose a piece of A5 paper and stick a people shape at the bottom of it. Write your name on the figure. Use a white crayon or candle to write 'Jesus' above the figure, and choose a paint colourwash to brush over the wax writing. Remember that he is always with you.

1 Peter 5:7

Cast all your anxiety on him because he cares for you.

You will need: plastic disposable cups; dried rice; small food bags; medium-sized balloons; scissors; permanent marker pens

Follow these instructions to make a stress ball. Half-fill a plastic cup with rice. Pour the rice into a food bag. Twist the bag and fold the excess plastic over, to form a ball shape.

Cut the neck off two balloons of different colours. Stretch one balloon over the rice bag, then stretch the other balloon over it, hiding the hole. Decorate with permanent marker pens.

Whenever you need to share a worry with God, use the stress ball while you talk with him. God is listening.

1 John 3:1
See what great love the Father has lavished on us, that we should be called children of God! And that is what we are!

  You will need: a Scrabble board and letter tiles

Use the Scrabble board and tiles to declare how you feel about God's love for you. Link the words if you wish.

Jeremiah 29:11
'For I know the plans I have for you,' declares the Lord, 'plans to prosper you and not to harm you, plans to give you hope and a future.'

  You will need: balls of play dough (see recipe on page 123); small food bags

Take a small piece of play dough and form a shape (whatever shape you choose) to say 'thank you' to God for everything he does for us. Put your shape into a bag to carry with you. Re-form your shape whenever there is a moment when you feel thankful to God for something.

Jeremiah 1:5

'Before I formed you in the womb I knew you, before you were born I set you apart; I appointed you as a prophet to the nations.'

You will need: cross tattoos or funky wrist tattoos (available from www.bakerross.co.uk); damp sponges

How amazing it is that God knew us even before we were born! Whatever we wear, or however we change ourselves, God only sees the real us. Put a cross tattoo on to your arm. When you look at it, remember that, however we look on the outside, God knows us because of what we are inside, including our strengths and weaknesses.

THEME: GOD LOVES YOU

Dear friends, let us love one another, for love comes from God.
Everyone who loves has been born of God and knows God.
1 JOHN 4:7

Nails love: John 3:16
For God so loved the world that he gave his one and only Son, that
whoever believes in him shall not perish but have eternal life.

You will need: small wooden blocks, each prepared with
twelve nails stuck in to form a 3D cross shape; balls of
wool; scissors

Wind wool around the nails to form a cross shape. God
gave us his only Son to take our sins all the way to the cross.

Knot love: Psalm 136:1
Give thanks to the Lord, for he is good. His love endures for ever.

You will need: photocopies of Celtic knot designs (see
templates on page 126); pencil crayons

Choose a Celtic knot to colour. Each knot is made from one
continual line, showing God's unending and boundless
love for each one of us.

Print love: 1 John 4:8

Whoever does not love does not know God, because God is love.

You will need: photocopies of the 'Love' print template (see page 127); pencil crayons

Robert Indiana created a 'Love' print in 1965. It became a Christmas card and a stamp design, and giant steel sculptural versions can now be spotted in many locations around the world. How big is God's love for you? Colour your own 'Love' print and give it to a loved one.

Bread love: Psalm 34:14

Turn from evil and do good; seek peace and pursue it.

You will need: printed peace symbols (see templates on page 128); sliced white bread; variety of food colourings; full fat milk; bowls; clean paintbrushes; electric toaster

God wants us to act in peace and love. Paint a slice of bread with a peace sign, using a mixture of milk and food colouring. Then toast the bread to set the colours.

Pretzel love: Ephesians 4:2

Be completely humble and gentle; be patient, bearing with one another in love.

You will need: pretzels; chocolate sauce; bowls

The pretzel shape shows us how people in the early church crossed their arms across their chest in prayer. In AD610, a monk baked pretzels as a reward for children who could recite prayers. Thank God for his love, dip a pretzel in chocolate sauce and eat it as a celebration of prayer.

Scrabble love: 1 Corinthians 13:13
And now these three remain: faith, hope and love. But the greatest of these is love.

You will need: a Scrabble board and letter tiles

Use the Scrabble board and letters to declare how you feel about God's love for you. Link the words if you wish.

Foam love: Ephesians 2:10
For we are God's handiwork, created in Christ Jesus to do good works, which God prepared in advance for us to do.

You will need: shaving foam; shallow trays or plates; acrylic paints; straws or wooden sticks; card heart or people shapes; a squeegee

Spray shaving foam on to a shallow tray or plate. Stir some drops of acrylic paint into the shaving foam and swirl with a stick or straw. Press a body or heart shape on to the coloured foam. Lift and leave for ten seconds. Scrape off excess foam with a squeegee, and look at the marbled design on your card shape. God created you unique: you will not match another person.

Neighbour love: Mark 12:31

'The second [commandment] is this: "Love your neighbour as yourself." There is no commandment greater than these.'

You will need: a large sheet of paper; pens

How do we measure love? By the many people we show love to. Across the top of the sheet of paper, write, 'Love your neighbour'. Then write 'your' 20 times down the left-hand side and 'neighbour' 20 times down the right-hand side. Think of a 'neighbour' whom God is calling you to pray for, and add them to the prayer sheet. Write their name or an adjective that describes them in some way. If you don't want to write it down, just say it quietly to yourself.

Feeder love: Luke 12:6

'Are not five sparrows sold for two pennies? Yet not one of them is forgotten by God.'

You will need: assorted chenille sticks; breakfast cereal hoops

MESSY PRAYER

Show God's love to the birds by making a bird feeder for the garden. Form a chenille stick into a heart shape, thread breakfast cereal hoops on to it, and twist the ends together.

PRAYER IDEAS FOR THE CELEBRATION TIME

PAPER BAG PRAYER

Take an ordinary paper bag, similar to a sweet shop bag. Open the bag, place your fingers around the neck and blow a few breaths into it. Whisper something you want forgiveness for into the bag. Blow up the bag with bigger breaths and, on a count of three, burst it by hitting it with your other hand, as a sign that God forgives you. This activity works very well, when it is clearly directed, with a large Messy congregation.

PAPER PLANE PRAYER

Everyone has their favourite instructions for folding a paper aeroplane. Create some planes as part of the activity hour, and write prayers on the wings, on the theme of the session. Ask everyone to take their planes into the celebration time and give them instructions on how to throw and where to aim all together. Throw the planes, after a countdown.

Pick up a plane that has landed close to you and read the prayers out loud to God.

CHURCH WINDOWS

Explore any stained-glass windows that your church building may have. See if any of them portray Bible stories that you hope to share over the coming year. Invite everyone to look at the windows and imagine where they might be in the stories they depict.

OBJECTS

Congregations love to hold objects to focus on together. You could use a teardrop shape to depict God's sadness about things happening in the world, or a heart shape, if the message is about God's love or relationships. A cross shape would be appropriate when talking about Jesus' death or forgiveness, a fish shape when talking about evangelism, or a door key to represent the persecuted church or a breakthrough in prayer.

IMAGINING

Encourage your Messy congregation to use their imagination. Tell a Bible story and halt at certain times to invite everyone to close their eyes. Who would they be in the story? What can they see? What can they hear? What can they smell? Ask everyone to open their eyes, and continue with the story.

At the end, invite the congregation to close their eyes again. Was there anything they noticed about the story, which took them by surprise?

DRAMA AND SINGING

'Freeze-frame' when acting out a story. Stop the drama at a point where you can ask the congregation to thank God or pray about something in the story. For example, at the point where Jesus is cooking for the disciples on the beach, thank God for the times when we share food with our friends, or thank God for the Messy cooks who prepare food for us each month.

Similarly, sing a song, such as 'We are marching in the light of God', while moving around the church or celebration space. Freeze in between verses and say a short prayer. Keep it lively!

POWERPOINT

PowerPoint images can be a powerful prayer tool. Reflective music, a photo on a screen, just one word, or a succession of slides—try it all. Use popular songs that can be appropriate to your theme, such as 'Footprints in the sand' sung by Leona Lewis, or Louis Armstrong's 'Wonderful world'.

AMEN!

Liven up the 'Amen' endings by winding up Amens with
your arm, shouting more and more loudly, or whizz around
on the spot, or try a Mexican wave 'Amen'.

LITURGICAL PRAYERS FOR THE CELEBRATION

LUCY MOORE

Lucy Moore is BRF's Messy Church team leader. She develops the work of Messy Church nationally and internationally, writing, speaking and developing projects.

When someone mentions 'liturgy', do you (a) groan, and protest that you belong to a Messy Church in order to escape such tedium? (b) start drooling in anticipation? (c) mutter to the person sitting next to you, 'Um, what does that mean, and will it hurt?'

The word 'liturgy' has a lot of baggage attached, and one of the fun things about Messy Church is the opportunity it provides to empty out baggage of all sorts, give it a good shake, spray it with air freshener and bin everything that's past its sell-by date. Then you can repack it, combining the old, treasured, unlosable, tried-and-tested classics of the past that will never go out of date with state-of-the-art, cutting-edge, spanking new kit. You end up with a bagful that, frankly, you wouldn't leave home without. Let's see what the traditional elements of liturgy look and sound like when they're placed in the gladiatorial arena of the Messy Church celebration.

Gladiatorial? Well, perhaps. For the early Christians—our brave brothers and sisters who had to face the ignominy and terror of martyrdom by the Romans—the arena was often the final testing place where the reality of their faith was exposed to the curious gaze of bloodthirsty onlookers. At some level, the spectators were asking, 'Is this a faith worth dying for?' For us, in softer times, the Messy celebration is the place where the reality of our communal faith is exposed to the view of onlookers who are not baying for our blood but, none the less, want to see what this Christianity is really all about. Is it a faith worth living for?

In the celebration, our words and actions, songs and prayers are either shown to have a whiff of eternity about them or exposed as empty shams. And the team leading the celebration needs to ask themselves, are they really worshipping God or simply putting on a show for others? Framed in those terms, Messy Church teams are among the bravest people in the land.

WHAT IS LITURGY?

One thing to place respectfully on the carpet is the fact that every church tradition has its liturgy. Some admit it more openly than others, and some have a more prescribed liturgy than others, but any gathering of people where there is an accepted way of behaving has already got a liturgy. So a liturgy might involve opening a prayer book to follow a service through or it might involve knowing that when the music group increases the volume and the words go up on the projector, we all stand up to sing. Human beings are hardwired for ritual. Liturgy is OK; it's a good thing. Let's make the most of it.

What sort of liturgy can you name in your church? And in your Messy Church?

Liturgy, according to the Church of England website, 'refers to the patterns, forms, words and actions through which public worship is conducted'. It comes from a Greek word and means 'work of [or *for* or *by*] the people'. Originally, in Greece, there was a system whereby wealthy people volunteered to pay for ceremonies that were of benefit to the rest of the state: 'liturgies' were religious ceremonies that included sporting events and days out at the theatre, but there were military 'liturgies' as well. Eventually it got too expensive and the system imploded—a solemn warning to us all not to overspend on our absolutions and to keep our thuribles under strict financial control! Seriously, though, 'liturgy' comes from a tradition in which those who were blessed with treasures willingly and voluntarily spent them for the benefit of people who had nothing, and this is a great image of what we do in corporate worship.

What are our 'treasures' in Messy Church, in the context of gathered worship? We have the glittering Gospels, the sparkling Psalms, and the gems of traditional, tried-and-tested prayers and patterns of worship. We have God-given imagination and Jesus' compassion on those who are lost and who are searching for him. Most of all, we have the Holy Spirit, like treasure in a jar of clay (2 Corinthians 4:7), who shines out in the faith we've been given in our own lives and makes all things new (Revelation 21:5). We also have jewel-like permission to try out *new* words and actions... or do we?

THE PROBLEM WITH LITURGY

A fundamental problem for many of us attending 'ordinary churches' week by week is that we don't see new people flocking to join us for our 'prescribed' or 'traditional' liturgical worship. If we did, we wouldn't have needed Messy Church and other fresh expressions of church in the first place, so something is out of kilter.

A single liturgy unites a denomination, perhaps. It may also serve the purpose of excluding heresy. The problem for us is that strict prescriptive rules about what is and isn't permitted can strangle new life and can quickly become meaningless to those who are unfamiliar with them. A prescribed and inflexible liturgy may unite only those who have already bought into it and may even encourage them to feel superior to those who are ignorant of it. Liturgy can easily find itself on one side of a chasm dividing the people who have always come to church from those who are only just starting to belong—those who are 'in' from those who are 'out'. Its language and actions can be incomprehensible and irrelevant to those finding faith for the first time, however dear it may be to those who are familiar with it.

It may prove a stumbling block if we insist that every newcomer, whatever their learning style, age, level of literacy or stage of faith, has to toe our liturgical line. And to be honest, as regards heresy, the danger is not really that Messy Church might become heretical, more that we might sell short the gospel by not risking any theology beyond the über-safe 'God is big and Jesus is our friend'.

Nevertheless, there are many riches within our set liturgies that could prove enriching and life-enhancing to newcomers, if only we can present them in such a way as to reveal their worth and relevance. We don't want to discard mindlessly everything in our traditions, out of fear that it's 'too complicated' or 'too old-fashioned'. A certain degree of 'mystery', too, can be intriguing and stimulating. So we need permission—indeed, we need encouragement—to reimagine the old and try out the new in a spirit of trust, accountability and mutual benefit.

Messy Church is a chance to use the old *and* the new in corporate worship, to refresh and reimagine the old and to risk experimenting with the new. This can be done in love and respect both for the living work of the Spirit in our time and for the church family to which we belong.

Are you more tempted to throw out the baby with the bathwater (getting rid of everything from your tradition, good and bad) or to hold on to the baby so tightly that you can't pick up its younger sibling (championing the old at the expense of the new)?

HOW SHOULD LITURGY BE DONE?

We also need to make it clear that, in the immortal words of Bananarama, 'It ain't what you do, it's the way that you do it.' The way we lead people into worship and go with them on the journey—if you like, the character that shines through our words and actions—is just as important as the liturgy we use in our worship.

New expressions of worship tend to be more spontaneous and informal than older 'set' acts of worship, which are arguably more robust and less dependent on the personality of individual leaders. In the words of a bishop who shall remain nameless, 'Any numpty can read a set service out of a book'—but any liturgy, old or new, can be led either with passion, care and meaning, or (in the words of Peter

Hall, founder of the Royal Shakespeare Company) as 'dead theatre'.

The 'stage management' of an act of worship is crucial. I don't mean the ability to put on a show; I mean the organisation, professionalism, attention to detail, pace, volume and flow that enable people to trust what is being said. We are human beings, praying in a world full of things that distract our senses. The most wonderful prayer in the world can end in anarchy and distress simply because nobody has organised the equipment needed, rehearsed the actions, thought about the number of people involved or, if it involves certain items, had a fire extinguisher to hand.

It's worth bearing in mind that liturgy might mean 'the work *of* the people', and one trait of Messy Church is that it encourages participation, with as much as possible coming from the families and as little as possible imposed by a leader. So it will be helpful to ask yourself, not 'How can I lead these people?' but 'How can these people lead each other? How can I help them bring *their* praise—not mine— to God?'

Who can you think of in your Messy Church family who would love to lead part of the celebration?

Elsewhere in this book, Jane has provided some wonderful creative prayer suggestions in new forms, as have countless writers in the *Get Messy!* magazine and Messy Church leaders in their own churches. I've been challenged, though, to take some of our traditional prayers and suggest ways in which we can appropriately and constructively work them into our Messy Church worship. I want to help us all start (or continue to develop) thinking about how to reimagine our beloved traditional liturgical prayers and prayer patterns for our beloved new Messy families.

Here are a few suggestions for reimagining liturgical prayer. This is by no means an exhaustive list, and I've used mainly Anglican examples simply because that's the tradition I'm most familiar with. Rather than inviting you to copy and paste these suggestions on to your PowerPoints for the next celebration, I want to inspire you to dig into the treasure chest of your own tradition's 'set prayers' and work out how you might offer them to your Messy families as an enriching tool for worship.

Which prayers do you love and how might you pass them on to Messy families so that they might love them too? For me, one would have to be the short prayer in the Evening Prayer service from the 1549 Book of Common Prayer:

Lighten our darkness, Lord, we beseech thee, and by thy great mercy defend us from all perils and dangers of this night, for the love of thy only Son, our Saviour, Jesus Christ.

It works for me for the following reasons:

- the association with my much-loved childhood village church

- its regular repetition throughout my childhood, which has put it in my long-term memory

- the link with a wider world of Christians in time and space, for whom night-time was or is really perilous

- its brevity in a service that contains some *really* long prayers and psalms

- its pleasing rhythm, which makes it almost like a poem

- its clear, practical but also symbolic request

I would happily share this prayer with my Messy family.

Pause for a moment and scribble down two or three of the phrases, prayers or actions that have come to mean a great deal to you over your time belonging to your church. Why have you chosen them?

CALL TO WORSHIP/GREETING

A request was put out on Facebook for Messy Church leaders to suggest a 'traditional prayer that you would like to pass on to your Messy Church families', and one response was the Choristers' Prayer:

Bless, O Lord, us Thy servants, who minister in Thy temple. Grant that what we sing with our lips, we may believe in our hearts, and what we believe in our hearts, we may show forth in our lives. Through Jesus Christ our Lord. Amen.

CHORISTERS' POCKET BOOK
(SCHOOL OF ENGLISH CHURCH MUSIC, 1934)

This is a good example of a prayer that we may dismiss out of hand for use within a Messy Church setting, as it includes a very definite 'thy' or two (shock, horror). The word order of its opening clause is rather clunky for modern ears, too: 'Bless, O Lord, us Thy servants…' But it's a beautifully balanced petition with a smooth, thought-provoking throughflow of ideas. Putting aside the theological question of whether we can equate a church building with 'Thy temple', it is essentially an appropriate request to make of God and a good reminder of the truth that we need to do more than just put on appearances in worship.

If you love this prayer and want to share it, how might you use it (or similar much-loved but slightly archaic prayers) in Messy Church? Here are some thoughts:

- You could use it as an introduction to the first song sung in the celebration every month. Just pray the prayer from the front, inviting everyone to join in as they learn the words. Launch straight into the song afterwards, perhaps omitting 'Through Jesus Christ our Lord. Amen', to avoid losing pace.

- Don't be afraid to shorten it. In this case, consider losing the first sentence.

- Add actions; this one suggests obvious hand movements for 'lips', 'hearts' and 'showing forth', which would be fun, aid concentration, slow down the speed of delivery and enhance the meaning of the words.

CONFESSION

Another favourite prayer, offered as a response to the same Facebook post, is the Jesus Prayer: 'Lord Jesus Christ, Son of the Living God, have mercy on me, a sinner.'

If your Messy congregation is suspicious of anything involving the unfashionable word 'sinner', you could give a little background to a prayer like this. Say that it's a really old prayer, which Christians all over the world have used since around AD400—so it's 1600 years old. It's the prayer spoken by the tax collector in Jesus' parable, who wasn't full of pride, unlike the other man praying in the story (Luke 18:10–14). Christians use the Jesus Prayer to 'still' themselves and enjoy spending time quietly just being with God.

During the celebration, try a short fun time of 'breathing' this prayer. Breathe in as the first phrase is spoken ('Lord Jesus Christ'), out on the second phrase ('Son of the Living God'), in again on the third phrase ('Have mercy on me') and out again on the last phrase ('a sinner'). Try it together a few times, with the leader speaking the words. Then try keeping the breathing rhythm, but without saying the words aloud. Instead, invite people to say the words in their head silently as they breathe.

Don't worry if people explode in giggles over their breathing efforts: human beings like to laugh. Suggest that this is a good prayer to use while you're waiting for a bus or in a supermarket queue (in your head rather than out loud).

PRAISE

Consider reworking the short sentences of praise in the 'call/response' type of prayer that we often use in traditional worship. Is there a phrase from the Bible story you've used as the theme for your Messy Church session that could be used as a prayer of praise? Could you adapt something that someone says to or about Jesus, or a phrase that picks up Jesus' own words?

For example, you might have been exploring Jesus' entry to Jerusalem. Here are some prayer lines with a response from Matthew 21:9:

Jesus came not to blame people but to rescue them.
Hosanna! God saves!
He rescued people from illness.
Hosanna! God saves!
He rescued them from fear.
Hosanna! God saves!
He rescued them from hate.
Hosanna! God saves!
He rescued them from death.
Hosanna! God saves!
He rescues us today from anything that keeps us away from him.
Hosanna! God saves!

Remember that it may be more powerful and inclusive to invite different individuals to pray the 'call' lines, rather than the usual leader.

Another inclusive approach might be to use a few prepared lines to set the tone of the prayer, then ask the congregation to suggest similar short prayers of praise from their own understanding of Jesus, with everyone else saying, 'Hosanna! God saves!' in response.

CREED

It may not be appropriate to use any form of the creed in Messy Church. It is appropriate in traditional church, where we can probably assume a certain level of Christian commitment and belief, or, at least, a willingness to go along with that belief. But in Messy Church we are deliberately trying to create a safe space for people of all beliefs and none to gather and see who Jesus Christ is, without being made to feel uncomfortable. A postmodern congregation is unlikely to say things they don't really believe simply because it's polite, and this is a good thing, so we don't want to put them in a position where they have to voice beliefs that they may not yet own. The big two—the Nicene Creed and the Apostles' Creed—contain beliefs for which Christians have died over the centuries, and we don't want to dilute the strength of these statements of belief. Most Messy Church congregations are not ready to say them.

COLLECTS

Similarly, collects (set prayers, written in a certain pattern of addressing God, describing him, asking him for something, saying why we want it and ending with praise) are unlikely to be appropriate for a monthly Messy Church, for the following reasons:

- The original purpose (to unite the church and perhaps to signal the end of corporate silent prayer) may have been lost in the mists of time through lack of reiteration.

- They are too wordy, with long, complicated sentence structures, resulting in a lack of clarity.

- They are difficult to memorise or internalise.

- They may have no connection with the theme of the service.

- They are difficult for all to participate in. (Because of their complexity, a good level of literacy is needed.)

- They are written in archaic language that often lacks any compensating beauty.

A prayer becomes well loved and gains the power to change our lives, often, because we repeat it until it sinks into the long-term memory and becomes part of who we are. The frequency of our meeting is a factor to consider when we try to discern what is practical and helpful to us in worship.

As a team, ask yourselves:

- How might you use different forms of prayer to unite your Messy Church with the rest of your church, denomination, Messy Church network, or global church?

- Do you do anything for reasons that now need explaining to your Messy congregation afresh?

- How wordy have you become, especially in the celebration? Are there other ways of communicating?

- How much do you rely on everyone being able to read or having English as their first language?

- Do you use some prayers and songs that you repeat often enough for people to 'own'?

- Do you follow through the theme well in all parts of Messy Church?

- Are there any parts of your session that have become too complex, long or needlessly intricate, and need simplifying?

- What is beautiful in your Messy Church?

SILENCE

Is silence a prayer? Of course! Unless we think of a conversation as being all one way. One of the greatest gifts that the church can provide to a hectic, noise-filled world is a space to be silent. Do you remember Screwtape's demonic loathing of 'music and silence' (C.S. Lewis, *The Screwtape Letters*)? There is something in silence that speaks of and to God without the need for words, and a communal silence can move people of all ages way beyond what we understand cerebrally, into holiness. Thomas Kelly wrote about the Quakers, 'In the Quaker practice of group worship on the basis of silence come special times when an electric hush and solemnity and depth of power steals over the worshippers… The Burning Bush has been kindled in our midst, and we stand together on holy ground' (*The Gathered Meeting*, Friends United Press, 1948).

However, as an all-age community, we need ways to frame silence. I was present at a Remembrance service when the minister launched into the two-minute silence with no explanation or introduction, to the confusion and therefore suppressed hilarity of the Cub Scouts present. Ouch! Try framing silence by:

- explaining what you're doing, why and for how long.

- using visuals. It can be helpful for people to have something to look at while they're being silent—for example, a picture, an object or a stained-glass window.

- playing music. This helps to make it clear that there will be a start and an end to the period of silence: it isn't going to go on for ever.

- using a simple invitation after a story, such as, 'Now, in your head, ask Jesus, "What do you want me to see in this story?" Which part of the story will he bring into your mind as you listen? I'll give you a moment of quiet to listen to him.' Signal the end of the silence by saying, 'Now, if you'd like to, tell the person you came with what you saw or heard while we were being quiet.'

- using a stilling exercise. Inviting everyone to listen quietly for 30 seconds to the sounds they can hear is a good way to prepare people for worship.

- using a simple prayer that introduces a moment of silence. For example, you might pray, 'Lord of wild winds and crackling flames, thank you for times that are *loud*. [Everyone shouts 'Yay!' or other words of praise and strums instruments.] Lord of breathing and of heartbeats, thank you for times that are *quiet*. [Everyone listens.]'

As a team, can you choose or devise a way of 'framing a time of silence' in the celebration, so that the repetition of the act of silence becomes a regular part of your worship and it becomes easier for everyone to enjoy it? Can you create a signal to indicate that a time of silence is about to happen (a countdown, a series of hand gestures or actions, a simple song, or something similar)?

When you look back at a Messy Church moment and someone says, 'When X happened, you could hear a pin drop', reflect on what was going on.

SUNG PRAYER AND PSALMS

Music is inseparably linked with time. All music exists within time, and is a shaping of time in sound. It heightens our awareness of sound and silence in a timeframe; it heightens our awareness of time. All worship exists within time, and is a shaping of time with prayer and praise.

JOHN HARPER, FROM A 2001 DRAFT FOR AN ARTICLE RELATED TO *PATTERNS FOR WORSHIP*

Here are some suggestions for ways of using music to enhance your prayer times.

- Play quiet music behind a spoken prayer.

- Pray by singing. The Fischy Music CD *Bring It All to Me* is beautifully constructed with plenty of 'call and response' versions of different psalms for many moods.

- Instead of using a whole psalm, carefully select some verses.

- As you develop favourite songs in Messy Church, use phrases, verses or couplets from them and from traditional hymns, not only as songs but also as spoken prayers. One favourite prayer mentioned in response to our Facebook question was actually a verse from a 1792 hymn by John Leland: 'Lord, keep us safe this night, secure from all our fears. May angels guard us while we sleep, till morning light appears.' A modern example of a song that is also a prayer is the quiet song 'Wonderful Lord, wonderful God' by Doug Horley.

THE LORD'S PRAYER

A prayer that we have used every time in our Messy Church is the Lord's Prayer. I have written about this elsewhere (in *Messy Church 3*), and you can see various versions of the actions we use on YouTube, but I've outlined them here, as they are proving very popular.

Our Father in heaven,
(Raise arms up high)

hallowed be your name.
(Trace a big perfect circle in front of you with your hands)

Your kingdom come, your will be done
(Slowly stretch out your arms to show the posture of Jesus on the cross)

on earth
(Still with arms outstretched, turn your palms to face down)

As in heaven.
(Still with arms outstretched, turn palms to face up)

Give us today our daily bread.
(Hold out your hands as if receiving bread)

LITURGICAL PRAYERS FOR THE CELEBRATION

Forgive us our sins

(Wipe your left hand with your right hand)

as we forgive those who sin against us.

(Wipe your right hand with your left hand)

And lead us not into temptation

(Make a fist and cross that arm across your chest)

but deliver us from evil.

(Make a fist with the other hand and cross that arm over your chest)

For the kingdom,

(Stretch out your arms as above, as if on the cross)

the power

(Make a strong 'muscley' pose with both arms)

and the glory are yours,

(Reach up and make your fingers come slowly down as if you're showing raindrops falling)

now

(Point to your left, with your left hand)

and for ever.

(With your right hand, make a spiralling movement from the left hand over towards the right, as far as you can go)

Amen

(Bring both palms above your head and clap)

MESSY GRACE

Our request for 'prayers from your tradition that you'd like to hand on to your Messy Church' revealed that the Grace is a firm favourite. When I shared the actions to the Messy Grace with a team planning their first Messy Church, it was glorious to see the spontaneous laughter and enjoyment evoked by simply praying this old prayer in a slightly new way. Needless to say, inviting anyone who knows it to come and help you lead it becomes a great way of building a non-hierarchical community as more and more families learn it.

If you have missed it in the Messy Church books so far, here are the actions:

May the grace of our Lord Jesus Christ,
(Hold out your hands as if you're offering a really big present, as that's what grace is like)

the love of God,
(Give yourself a hug)

and the fellowship of the Holy Spirit
(Join hands with the people next to you)

be with us all evermore. Amen
(On 'Amen', lift your joined hands up high)

MESSY BLESSINGS

A blessing is a beautiful gift for the church to offer families. There is a peculiar power in asking one of the congregation to say the words of blessing, rather than assuming that they need to be spoken by you or another leader. You might give someone the words to read or invite them to devise their own, maybe looking through some Bible verses to find one that they like best.

Here are a few suggestions, but you could also look at the passage used in your Messy Church session to see if any of it might be turned into a blessing prayer.

- The Lord bless you and keep you; the Lord make his face to shine upon you, and be gracious to you; the Lord lift up his countenance upon you, and give you peace (Numbers 6:24–26, NRSV).

- The Lord will keep you from all harm—he will watch over your life; the Lord will watch over your coming and going both now and for evermore (Psalm 121:7–8).

- Peace I leave with you; my peace I give you. I do not give to you as the world gives. Do not let your hearts be troubled and do not be afraid (John 14:27).

- The God of peace be with you all. Amen (Romans 15:33).

- Grace and peace to you from God our Father and the Lord Jesus Christ (1 Corinthians 1:3).

- Finally, brothers and sisters, rejoice! Strive for full restoration, encourage one another, be of one mind, live in peace. And the God of love and peace will be with you (2 Corinthians 13:11).

- The grace of our Lord Jesus Christ be with your spirit, brothers and sisters. Amen (Galatians 6:18).

- I keep asking that the God of our Lord Jesus Christ, the glorious Father, may give you the Spirit of wisdom and revelation, so that you may know him better (Ephesians 1:17).

- Rejoice in the Lord always. I will say it again: rejoice! Let your gentleness be evident to all. The Lord is near. Do not be anxious about anything, but in every situation, by prayer and petition, with thanksgiving, present your requests to God. And the peace of God, which transcends all understanding, will guard your hearts and your minds in Christ Jesus (Philippians 4:4–7).

There are some lovely Celtic blessings available, from which you might just pick a phrase or two in the Messy context. (Search online for Celtic blessings to find some that are most appropriate for your context.) Celtic prayers work well for Messy families, perhaps because they are rooted in the natural world and tangible things around us.

The following traditional prayer is beautiful and the first and / or last phrases alone might be used as a blessing:

May the blessing of light be upon you,
light on the outside,
light on the inside.

With God's sunlight shining on you,
may your heart glow with warmth,
like a turf fire
that welcomes friends and strangers alike.

May the light of the Lord shine from your eyes,
like a candle in the window,
welcoming the weary traveller.
TRADITIONAL, AUTHOR UNKNOWN

MESSY PEACE

The peace of the Lord be always with you.
And also with you.
Let's offer one another a sign of peace.

This simple prayer for peace, accompanied by a handshake, is very usable in Messy Church just as it is, but you might want to refresh it and have more fun with it, by turning it into a game.

Games are full of rituals and rules. Like dance and theatre, they go very well with liturgy. (Cerys Hughes, Messy Church Adviser for Lichfield Diocese, invented the Messy Can-Can Can, turning the church collection into a game played by passing a collecting can around the congregation within the span of the Can-Can tune—53 seconds, apparently. This is a good example of liturgy reinvented appropriately and providing great engagement with the liturgical act of giving for all ages.)

Give everyone a small piece of card printed with a dove, the symbol of peace. Invite everyone to go round and give someone else their dove as they say the words of the Peace. They listen to the response and perhaps receive a dove back if the person they're speaking to happens to have one. Then they each go and offer someone else the dove of peace, and so on, for an appropriate length of time. The prayer for each other becomes a game in the best sense.

You might want to explain that the Hebrew concept of *shalom* ('peace') means much more than just 'peace and quiet': what we're really praying for is 'life in all its fullness' (John 10:10, GNB).

The Peace is a very suitable prayer to be led by someone from the congregation rather than always an ordained minister.

Similarly, once you've all learned it, you could ask a child or other congregation member to lead a dismissal, such as:

Go in peace to love and serve the Lord.
In the name of Christ. Amen

This dismissal might be used regularly at the end of the meal rather than at the end of the celebration, to finish the whole Messy Church session by sending people out into the rest of the day in peace and with a purpose.

CONCLUSION

These are just a few examples to start your imagination running. In summary:

- Think and pray together about what 'treasures' from your tradition you want to share with your Messy families.

- Wherever possible, let the congregation lead, devise, create and participate.

- See your liturgy as a game, not an ordeal.

- Explain anything that might be unclear.

- Add actions.

- Add music.

- Add visuals.

- Shorten prayers if they contain unnecessary words.

- Most of all, remember that this is our worship, not a show that we lay on for others.

Which part of this challenge do you feel most excited about?

PRAYER IDEAS FOR THE MEAL TIME

Meal times at Messy Church can be an opportunity for more than just eating. They provide a crucial time for conversations and further exploration of the theme for the session. Activities can continue throughout the meal time and right up until the families depart.

During the first course, you could engage in 'table talk' time, when simple 'I wonder' questions are asked and families can discuss together. Maybe you could print the questions on to paper, or, if you have a microphone, ask them out loud. The *Get Messy!* magazine includes 'Mealtime cards', with suggestions for each monthly session.

When do you celebrate birthdays at your Messy Church? The time when everyone is eating together is an excellent opportunity. Do you give out birthday bags to all ages? If so, what do you include in the bags—a birthday card, a chocolate bar, or bubble mixture? Perhaps they could contain a Messy Church prayer card to take home. What would you put on such a card, and how would it look?

At L19: Messy Church, we have had great success with something that we call 'MESSages to God'. This form of praying is easy and appeals to all ages. While the dessert or cakes are being served at the tables, we invite helpers to be prayer monitors. The children never hesitate to volunteer, and they dash about the dining area giving out pencils and very small squares of coloured paper. People write a prayer clearly on the paper and post it into an empty tissue box. I then take home the box and write up all of the prayers in an email. (People are asked to add their name if they want it typed alongside their prayer.)

We are still surprised, every month, that so many Messy families want to engage in this experience of talking to God. When I type out the prayers, I discover a huge need for healing. Many people are better able to write down their needs for prayer than to share them verbally or in silence with God.

We need as many varieties of ways to help our Messy families talk to God as possible. In the 'MESSages to God' email to the L19 congregation, I suggest that they read the prayers and then pray them loudly or quietly, in the house or in the park, whenever they can, between the monthly Messy Church sessions. I also email the prayers to key pray-ers in the other church congregations and prayer groups, so that they can pray too. One month, I was unable to get to my computer to write up the prayers, as I was travelling straight to different accommodation. Upon my return, I found I had received emails from people asking if they had missed the 'MESSages to God'.

GRACES

In the Lord's Prayer, Jesus taught us to pray, 'Give us today our daily bread' (Matthew 6:11).

Jesus blessed the bread and the fishes when he fed the 5000. For some families, it is a regular practice to pray thanks for a meal before eating. Others, unfamiliar with graces, may enjoy being introduced to some lively versions at Messy Church. I do not know the source of all the graces below, but many of them are used by the Scout and Guide organisations.

God, you're great!
God, you're good!
And we thank you for our food.
We're gonna thank you morning, noon and night,
we're gonna thank you 'cos you're dynamite!
Amen! (clap, clap)
Amen! (clap, clap)
Amen! (clap, clap)
SUNG TO THE TUNE OF 'ROCK AROUND THE CLOCK'

MESSY PRAYER

Thanks a lot for our food, Lord,
thanks a lot for our food.
We all love you a lot, Lord,
thanks a lot for our food.
Amen.
SUNG TO THE TUNE OF 'TIE ME KANGAROO DOWN, SPORT'

Da da da da (click, click)
Da da da da (click, click)
Da da da da, da da da da, da da da da, (click, click)
We really are so grateful
for all that's on our plateful [or, 'on our table'],
for all of your creation
and all our family.
Da da da da (click, click)
Da da da da (click, click)
Da da da da, da da da da, da da da da.
Amen
SUNG TO THE TUNE OF 'THE ADDAMS FAMILY'

Top nosh! The most incredible
Top nosh! That's ever fed to me.
Breakfast through till dinner and tea,
all my friends can share it with me.

Top nosh! So tasty it could be
Straight from heaven above.

PRAYER IDEAS FOR THE MEAL TIME

Thank you, God, as you guide
and for all you provide —
food and fellowship… and love!
SUNG TO THE TUNE OF 'TOP CAT'

Thank you, Lord, for all of our food.
Thank you, Lord, for all of our food.
For daily bread,
for things you said.
Thank you, Lord, for all of our food.
SUNG TO THE *SUPERMAN* THEME

ABCDEFG
Thank you, God, for feeding me.

Lord, bless this bunch
as they eat this lunch.

321, 123,
thank you, Lord, for this tea.

PRAYER IDEAS TO USE IN THE HOME

Messy Churches often hear about families who enjoy taking home prayer pebbles or prayer boxes that they have made together at their local Messy Church. But what happens next? What happens when the family returns home?

On your 'take-home' sheets at Messy Church, you could add the following websites for families to explore together:

- www.faithinhomes.org.uk

- www.godventure.co.uk/category/prayer-activities

- www.going4growth.org.uk/growth_in_faith_and_worship/prayer

- www.flamecreativekids.blogspot.co.uk

- www.prayerspacesinschools.com

- www.barnabasinchurches.org.uk/find/prayer/ideas/1

- www.prayerrequest.com

Here are some more ideas for encouraging prayer to continue at home.

- Choose a windowsill for the purpose of prayer and set it up with prayer items, such as a variety of crosses and candles. A plastic teaspoon with 'tsp' written in permanent marker is a good prayer prompt. It reminds us to thank God, say sorry or say please. The windowsill could be a place to display any Messy Church crafts or pictures. Write or draw prayers on small pieces of paper and place them inside a jar or container. When the jar is full, empty the contents on to a table and read them. Have any of the prayers been answered? Expand on the 'tsp' idea for younger children by making three large paper envelopes to hang on the windowsill. Each envelope could be decorated with one of the 'tsp' letters in a grand way. Invite children to post prayers inside the large envelopes.

- Spend an afternoon making some prayer cards together. Who would like to know that you are praying for them? Pop a prayer card through this person's door, or send it to them in the post.

- Find a box to hold photos. Do you have any friends or family who live a distance away? Find a photo of them and place it in the box. Every morning, choose one photo to place on top of the box. Ask God to care for that person during the day.

A MESSY CHURCH SESSION ON PRAYER

Theme: encouraging prayer
Biblical story: choose from the many occasions in the Bible when Jesus and his disciples prayed
Equipping today's families: there are lots of ways to pray and God is always listening. We can share each day with God and develop good prayer habits.

ACTIVITIES

1. PLAYCHUTE PRAYERS

You will need: a playchute and space to use it; a small ball

Sit all ages around a playchute. Choose a well-known tune, such as 'Frère Jacques' or a nursery rhyme. Invite everyone to take turns to sing just one word, one after another, to make up a new prayer. After a few lines, everyone stands and holds the playchute at waist height with their right hand. Move round together in a clockwise direction, chanting,

'For where two or three come together in my name…'; then, lift the playchute as high as possible, shouting, 'There am I with them.'

End with a Mexican wave 'Amen', using the playchute. Try rolling a small lightweight ball around the edge of the playchute as you slowly say 'Amen', starting quietly and building up to a loud shout.

Talk about

'For where two or three gather in my name, there am I with them' (Matthew 18:20). How confident are we that Jesus listens to our prayers? Does it make any difference whether we pray on our own or together with others?

2. GRAFFITI PRAYERS

You will need: white wallpaper lining; black sugar paper; masking tape; coloured chalks; white chalks; paints; paintbrushes; marker pens; old newspapers; glue; scissors

Prepare a wall of alternating black and white strips of paper, using masking tape to secure them. Write the heading 'It's not fair!' and invite responses to be written or drawn, using a variety of chalks, paints and pens provided. You could also cut out newspaper headings and stick them on the wall. Stand back and pray about all of the injustices in the world.

Invite a Messy Church team member to take a photograph of the completed graffiti prayer wall and email it to your Messy team and congregation. Use social media to promote further prayers by posting the photo on Facebook or Twitter.

Talk about

How can we help when things are unfair? Do we know enough about the facts of the matter? Who are the people who can make better decisions? How can we spread God's hope and love into these situations?

3. TSP PRAYERS

You will need: plastic teaspoons; permanent markers; paper napkins; felt-tipped pens; decorating stickers

Use a permanent marker to write 'TSP' on a plastic spoon. Open a napkin and write in each square quarter, as headings, 'Thank you', 'Sorry', 'Please' and 'Amen'. Write or draw some things to pray for in the first three quarters of the napkin. In the 'Amen' quarter, write some words that mean the same thing, such as 'I agree' or 'truly'. Decorate with stickers and drawings. Roll up the teaspoon in the napkin.

Talk about

In a cooking recipe, there is often an ingredient measured by a teaspoon. What do we need to add to a prayer? Prayers don't need to be big. A small teaspoon prayer is really useful and can be very powerful.

4. EDIBLE HEART PRAYERS

You will need: slices of wholemeal bread; heart-shaped cookie cutters; red jam; food wrap bags

Cut out two heart shapes from bread and sandwich them together with jam. Wrap them in a bag and take home to eat later.

Talk about

'I call with all my heart; answer me, Lord, and I will obey your decrees' (Psalm 119:145). God wants us to pray with our whole hearts. It isn't just about what we can do for God, but also about how we can work with God and be powerful in God's love together. How can we grow in God's love?

5. ARROW PRAYERS

You will need: strong paperclips; pliers; electrical or duct tape; rubber bands; plastic drinking straws; scissors

Use the pliers to open out a paperclip. Bend it into the shape of an archer's bow, and wind some tape around the whole bow to add strength. Bend back each end to make 'V' shaped hooks. Attach a rubber band to the two 'V' ends, making sure it stretches taut. Wrap a small piece of tape around the centre of the rubber band 'string', where the arrow will be placed.

To make two arrows, cut the bendy end off a drinking straw, and cut the remaining straight end in half. On each half, cut a slit through both sides of one end, to sit on the string. Wrap a small piece of tape around the other end to add weight. Place the slit end on the tape on the string, pull back and fire.

Talk about

The king said to me, 'What is it you want?' Then I prayed to the God of heaven, and I answered the king, 'If it pleases the king and if your servant has found favour in his sight, let him send me to the city in Judah where my fathers are buried so that I can rebuild it.' (Nehemiah 2:4–5)

Arrow prayers are the sort that you shoot up to God quickly at any time, anywhere. They are usually quite short in length, such as, 'Help me, God.' Have you ever asked God to help you like this, in a flash?

6. LOVE IN ACTION PRAYERS

You will need: photocopies of an action list (see below); 'ker-pow' images for reference; colouring pens

'Prayer in action is love; love in action is service,' said Mother Teresa. Love is nothing if it is not put into action. Write an action list: some examples are as follows.

- Help your family by making your bed.

- Send a 'Thinking of you' card to someone.

- Offer to babysit for a parent needing a break.

- Make breakfast for a busy person.

- Collect coupons or vouchers and give them to someone else.

- Purchase vegetable seeds to grow for someone else.

- Make a small 'goody' bag for a housebound person in your community.

- Sponsor a child in need overseas.

- Fill a shoebox with gifts of love for Operation Christmas Child.

- Make a bird feeder for the garden birds.

- Offer some help to a busy person.

- Choose a new charity to support for twelve months.

Read through your list and add any extra ideas you can think of. Choose four to put into action, as an individual or a family, and draw 'ker-pow' images alongside them. Colour in the images when the action is completed. At the bottom of the list, draw an extra large 'ker-pow' image and write 'God' in the centre. When all four actions have been completed, colour in the larger image.

Talk about

'Dear children, let us not love with words or speech but with actions and in truth' (1 John 3:18). How can we show God's unconditional love to others? What else could we add to the list?

7. CANDLE PRAYERS

You will need: tealights; votive glasses; glass paints; thin paintbrushes; small pieces of coloured tissue paper; PVA glue; glow sticks; glass jars with lids; scissors; rubber gloves

Choose which kind of candle holder you would like to make—a glass painted votive, a tissue mosaic votive (sticking tissue paper to the glass), or a glow stick lantern.

With glass painting, remember that less is more. When glueing tissue pieces on the glass, glue them to the outside.

For the glow stick lanterns, snap a glow stick (or several sticks in various colours) and cut them into pieces with scissors over a jar, to collect the inner fluid. (Use rubber gloves to protect yourself.) Place a lid tightly on the jar and shake so that the sides of the jar are coated with the glow stick fluid. Place in a dark room and enjoy the glow.

All these candle and glow stick crafts must be supervised by an adult.

Talk about

'I am the light of the world. Whoever follows me will never walk in darkness, but will have the light of life' (John 8:12). Lighting a candle is, in itself, a prayer. It is a sign of God's presence among us, a light in the darkness. 'Votive' means an offering. Who would you like to offer a candlelight prayer for?

8. JIGSAW PRAYER

You will need: a used jigsaw puzzle (most charity shops have supplies); a tray; envelopes; pencils

Spread the jigsaw pieces on to the tray and choose a piece. On an envelope, draw around the jigsaw piece and write your name alongside. Pop the jigsaw piece inside the envelope and take it home.

Talk about

'He is before all things, and in him all things hold together' (Colossians 1:17). Jesus is in control. Many of our prayers are about things we need help with. We can feel alone and helpless, or angry and confused. But God sees each one of us as a member of his special loving family. We all fit together in his puzzle, with no missing pieces, as he created each one of us individually and loves us so much that he knows the completed jigsaw picture. He knows where we are in his picture. We don't even need to know; we need only to trust that he is holding all of the jigsaw pieces, me and you.

Are we willing to let God hold the pieces of our lives?

9. SHREDDING PRAYERS

You will need: manual or electric paper shredder; recycled scraps of paper or old newspapers; pens or pencils; bin bags

What do we need to ask God's forgiveness for? To be in a good place with God, we need to confess our sins to him regularly. Whether it seems like a big or little thing to us, to God it is just a wrongdoing.

Write or draw your wrongdoing on some paper, or find a newspaper headline or story that expresses your need to ask for forgiveness. Place the paper in the shredder and, at the same time, say 'sorry' to God. Save the shredded paper in bin bags and reuse it in another Messy activity, such as a treasure dip or 'hide the sheep' activity.

Talk about

'Be kind and compassionate to one another, forgiving each other, just as in Christ God forgave you' (Ephesians 4:32). God loves us so much that he will forgive us when we share our sins with him, but sometimes this is hard to do.

Not only does unforgiveness come between us and God, but it also breaks our relationships with others. When Jesus was dying on the cross, he said, 'It is finished.' The original word, in the Greek language, means 'paid in full'. If we love Jesus, then our sins are removed.

10. JENGA PRAYER

You will need: giant or original Jenga blocks; pieces of paper; pens; sticky tack

Write the prayer prompt 'Please', 'Sorry' or 'Thank you' on to small pieces of paper and stick them on a few of your Jenga blocks. Then build a prayer tower up to God.

When playing the game, if you choose to remove a prayer block, respond with a short prayer before continuing. The winner is the last person to remove a block without making the tower fall.

Talk about

We are on the edge of our seats in anticipation when we play Jenga. It's exciting! When we pray to God, are we confident and bold or are we weak and struggling? God gets excited when we pray to him.

CELEBRATION

Bible story: Acts 9:36–42

TALK

What do you do when you make friends with someone? Do you talk to them? Do you spend time with them? Do you discover their likes and dislikes? Do you get to know all about them? Well, we can have Jesus as a friend like that, but he already knows all about us. After all, he did make us.

Have you ever seen smoke in church? What did it look like? It could have been incense. The burning of incense for worship and prayer goes back many years, and in the book of Exodus Moses is told to build an altar from wood on which incense can be burned. Moses was also given a formula to blend ingredients to make incense for burning.

The rising smoke was considered to be an offering to God, like prayers lifting high.

But today we will use bubbles—much safer and much more fun. Let's practise. If I give some to you… and you… whenever I say the word 'pray' or 'prayer', you can blow some bubbles up to God.

In the book of Acts, there are some miracles. One that stands out for me is in Acts 9:36–42. It happened to a disciple called Tabitha (also known as Dorcas), who was always doing good and helping the poor. She became sick and died, so her body was washed and placed in an upstairs room by her family and friends. But instead of praying themselves, they called for Peter, one of Jesus' first disciples, who was nearby. 'Please come at once,' they said.

When Peter arrived at the upstairs room, he sent everyone out, got down on his knees and prayed. He turned to the dead woman and said, 'Tabitha, get up.' She opened her eyes, saw Peter and sat up. When she had been helped to her feet, Peter presented her to everyone, alive! This became known all over the land and many people came to know Jesus.

Peter's prayer wasn't long or full of important words. He just said, 'Tabitha, get up.' Three little words, but a *big* prayer! *[Get out a bubble wand to blow a big bubble.]* It was simple but powerful. Peter had first prayed to God, on his knees. We don't know what he prayed or how long he prayed, but afterwards he just said three words: 'Tabitha, get up.' Peter knew Jesus and had spent time with him. He'd seen Jesus do miracles and heal the sick. He had faith in Jesus.

So we too must have faith and pray to God, often. Have faith, because God loves us enough to be with us in the good times and the bad. Share those times with him by praying—talking to him. Send your prayers up to him now. [*Blow bubbles.*]

Lord, we thank you for the awesome things you did and continue to do. Help us to be awesome for you and share our lives with you daily in prayer. As we watch the bubbles, we remember how your disciples prayed together after you left them. Yet you never really leave us. Friends are for ever. Amen

SONG SUGGESTIONS

- Do not worry (Doug Horley)

- May you find peace (Fischy Music)

- As we go now (Fischy Music)

A QUIET DAY: PRAYING WITH YOUR TEAM

There comes a time in your Messy Church development when you've been going for a while and fatigue starts to set in, along with a hint of a blasé attitude. Things might have settled, through nobody's fault, into a bit of a routine. Those on the fringes of the team may feel disconnected and those at the centre may feel exhausted. There is no forum for new ideas to be shared and no time for reflection on the 'ruts' that have begun to appear. The temptation to go through the motions becomes stronger each month and a corresponding sense of dissatisfaction is growing.

Here's a suggestion for a 'Messy Morning' to allow a team of all ages to reconnect, reinspire, reimagine and revive itself— and to have some really great family fun together. The aim is to give the whole Messy team space to pray, listen to God, talk together about ways to improve Messy Church and to feel appreciated by enjoying hands-on activities and food together.

OUTLINE

Approximate timings might be:

- 10.00   gather for brunch
- 10.30   activities carousel
- 11.30   celebration
- 12.00   lunch
- 1.00   depart

The theme for the activities is the five values of Messy Church (Christ-centred, All-age, Celebration, Creativity and Hospitality).

You will need:
- Delicious 'snacky' breakfast foods, such as doughnuts, pancakes, croissants, Danish pastries and fruit, as well as coffee, tea and juice
- Bowls of healthy snacks scattered around the stations to nibble, such as grapes, celery sticks, bread sticks, carrot sticks and raisins
- A fun lunch, such as fish and chips or other takeaway, with drinks (organised or ordered in advance)
- Five activity stations, as described below, with instructions and materials set out on the tables
- A bell or other signal

Invite everyone to arrive for brunch at 10.00 am and, over refreshments, explain the aim of the day (see above). Divide them into groups of roughly the same size (no more than five groups in total) and describe how each group will stick together and have ten minutes at each activity station, with a few minutes to change between stations. A bell or other signal will be sounded at the end of the ten minutes. Then each group will move to the next station until everyone has done every activity. It's helpful to have a leader at each station but it isn't obligatory.

After the activities, gather everyone together for a celebration: sing a favourite song, share Communion, if that's appropriate, and, instead of a Bible story, ask the groups to share any insights they've gained from doing the activities. These might be new understandings of God or new ideas for use in Messy Church or something completely different. Choose a prayer (from this book, perhaps), say 'thank you' for the food you're about to share and have lunch together.

ACTIVITIES

CHRIST-CENTRED

You will need: print-out of Luke 19:1–10; a person outline to represent Jesus, drawn on a large sheet of paper; pens in different colours

Together, read Luke 19:1–10.

Talk about what each of you sees as the main aspect of Jesus' character shown in this passage. Inside the outline of the figure of Jesus, write or draw the words you've mentioned. For example, someone might write inside the outline that in this story Jesus was observant.

Then talk about how your Messy Church might demonstrate this character trait in what you do there. Outside the figure of Jesus, write or draw your suggestions. For example, you might write that it would be good to have somebody in your Messy Church whose job it is to notice people who need a pastoral chat.

The next group to do this activity can continue adding insights and suggestions to those that the first group has put down.

ALL-AGE

You will need: a printed list of discipleship images, as below; assorted junk materials for modelling; sticky tape; card; scissors

Choose from the list below (or one of your own) the image that speaks loudest to your group about what a disciple is most like.

- An athlete
- A limb of a body
- A slave
- A mirror
- A soldier
- A partygoer
- A pilgrim
- A building under construction
- A sheep
- A family member

Together, make a model that represents this image.

Ask yourselves: how might this activity have been different if there had been other age groups, language groups or ability groups present?

CELEBRATION

You will need: coloured pens or crayons; a prepared poster with the word 'CELEBRATE!' and sketched outlines of items such as balloons, streamers, cake, a Communion cup and bread, trumpets and similar festive items

Colour in the poster together and add your own pictures for others to colour in. As you do so, talk about what or who you celebrate in your Messy Church and how you go about celebrating.

In the final few minutes, choose one detail of the bigger picture to pray about in one-word prayers.

CREATIVITY

You will need: good-quality pencils; erasers; paper; water; paints; paintbrushes

Each person works on their own for this activity. Choose one of the following questions and paint your answer on a sheet of paper, using any of the materials provided:

- If Messy Church were a **machine**, what would it look like?

- If Messy Church were a **tree**, what would it look like?

- If Messy Church were a **person**, what would it look like?

- If Messy Church were a **planet**, what would it look like?

- If Messy Church were an **animal**, what would it look like?

Talk about your designs in your group. Do the paintings spark off any ideas for your Messy Church?

HOSPITALITY

You will need: hand-washing facilities; flour; prepared bread dough (with a gluten-free option, if necessary); baking sheets; an oven; wire racks for cooling

Knead the dough and make plaited rolls together. As you do so, talk about what 'welcome' means, and how well you think you do it in your Messy Church.

After the celebration, when every group has done the activity, bake all the rolls and eat them with lunch. You may wish to label the rolls in some way when they go into the oven, so that people can identify the rolls they have made.

MESSY RETREAT: GOING AWAY TOGETHER

CERYS HUGHES AND LIZZIE HACKNEY

Cerys Hughes is the Messy Church Adviser for the Diocese of Lichfield, and Lizzie Hackney runs Dovedale House, the Children and Youth Retreat Centre of the Diocese of Lichfield. Dovedale House is part of the St Chad's Retreat Centres, which seek to be child-centred, mission-focused, intergenerational and Holy Spirit-led. Cerys and Lizzie are passionate about creating space for families to feel God's presence in their Messy lives.

There is something spiritually significant in the decision to leave one physical space for another as we seek time with God: Jesus himself often did it (see Luke 5:16; 22:39). Whether on retreats, pilgrimages, holidays (originally 'holy days') or prayer days, Christians have always engaged with the idea of 'going away' in order to worship God through a sacrifice of time and energy, and to connect with God in both fresh and old ways. They have gone away as individuals, but they have also gone as families and whole communities.

Jesus grew up in a culture that celebrated the exodus—God's love shown through family, community and journey. These themes influenced the way his people worshipped and engaged with God. Luke's account of Jesus visiting the temple when he was twelve years old (Luke 2:41–51) provides us with a fascinating glimpse into the joyful, if somewhat chaotic, intergenerational holiday experience of travelling en masse from Galilee to Jerusalem for the Passover meal.

Going away for a whole-day retreat helps families to disengage from the daily routine and focus on 'being' together. With all its fun, space, quietness and noise, the retreat becomes a prayer journey with God.

A RHYTHM

More time means more experiences, but also more spaces for engagement with God. If your Messy Church is going away for a day, a balanced programme is important. There need to be times when everyone is gathered together, times when smaller groups can engage with each other and opportunities for individuals to spend time with God.

When putting together a programme, meals and celebrations are the best framework for structuring the day. Here is a timetable that we have used.

- 10:00   Messy breakfast

- 10:30   Welcome, Messy morning prayers and storytelling

- 11:00   Messy creations

- 12:00   Midday Messy prayer

- 12:30   Lunch

- 13:30   Optional activities, walks, games and music

- 14:30   Messy Celebration

- 15:00   Close

Encourage everyone to use the time as they need and not to feel that they have to do everything.

A PLACE

Here are some questions to think about when you are deciding where to go for your Messy retreat.

- How much space (and how many spaces) might we need?

- Will we be spending time outdoors? Do we need wet weather options and what might they be?

- How far away is the venue? How will we get there? Will people travel together or meet there?

- Will we be taking our own food or visiting a place that provides food?

- Will there be a fixed cost or a request for donations, or will the venue be offered free?

- Is it a place where we can relax, and a place where all ages are welcome? (This is one of the most important questions.)

You may choose a place according to its spiritual significance, natural beauty or heritage. We have found it helpful to be aware of a place's 'identity'. We held a Messy retreat in Ilam in the Peak District, a place of pilgrimage associated with a Saxon prince from Stafford who travelled to Ilam and became a hermit and prayer warrior. His life story is very colourful and we chose to tell it during the day, highlighting how our stories connect with God's story. In a beautiful part of the country, surrounded by hills, streams and many sheep, we also chose to focus on Psalm 23.

Taking the time to reflect on what the place has to offer means that your themes are reinforced by the environment. Despite all our 'hard planning' for the retreat in Ilam, we found that God had the last word, as individuals experienced God speaking to them through the place and their time within it.

IDEAS FOR MESSY PRAYER

If you are the only group using your venue, you will have the freedom to create reflective prayer spaces that can be used throughout your time together, by families, groups or individuals. Some great ideas can be found at www.prayerspacesinschools.com.

Regular Messy prayer times can give structure to the day. Here are some suggestions for prayer times to 'punctuate' your time together.

MESSY MORNING PRAYERS

- Have a morning BBQ and cook a fish breakfast, as Jesus did after his resurrection (John 21:1–14). Talk about how Jesus has come to meet with us, and pray that we will all welcome him into our day.

- Ask everyone to bring a favourite book with them and invite people to read the beginning of their story. Talk about what makes a good story and ask others to share their hopes for your time together. Give everyone a notebook in which to write or draw their story of their time away. Pray for the day ahead and make space to share some new stories together at the end of your retreat.

MESSY NOONDAY PRAYERS

- Use spinning tops to reflect on the activity of life. God is the great 'starter' of activity and he holds us together. Pray about the things that we do, before the spinning tops fall.

- Cover your meal table with lining paper and encourage everyone to talk about the things they would like to thank God for or pray for over lunch. Encourage everyone to write or draw their ideas on the table covering, creating a visual image of prayer conversation as time is spent together. You could place prompts for ideas around the table in the form of images, questions or Bible verses.

MESSY EVENING PRAYERS

- Empty the contents of glow sticks into empty jars. Seal them and think about God's light in our lives. Pray for those who feel that they are in dark places.

- Use some of your favourite worship songs from your Messy Church. Have party food and party games to celebrate your time together.

MESSY NIGHT PRAYERS

- If you are still on retreat at night time, do some stargazing. Look at the stars and talk about how God knows each of us, just as he knows the stars: 'He determines the number of the stars and calls them each by name' (Psalm 147:4). Pray for everyone in your group by name.

- Have a feast using foods mentioned in the Bible, such as honey (Psalm 19:10), bread (Matthew 4:4) and fruit (1 Samuel 30:11–12), as well as water (John 4:13). Reflect on what it feels like to eat these foods and what they say to us about God's story.

Set in Ilam, a place of pilgrimage in the stunning Peak National Park, Dovedale House offers affordable accommodation for all. Mark and Lizzie run regular retreats for Messy Churches, families and leaders. There is information at www.dovedalehouse.org, or you can 'like' them on Facebook to find out how to take a group or book on to their events.

APPENDIX

BUBBLE MIXTURE

You will need:

- 500 ml soap (bubble bath or washing-up liquid)
- 250 ml glycerin (available from pharmacists)
- 5 litres water

To scale up or down, quantities are one part soap, half a part glycerin and ten parts water. Use a builders' tray to contain the bubble mixture.

You can make your own small bubble wands out of chenille sticks. For a much bigger option, use a hula hoop wrapped in string (it will work best with rough edges).

Bubble mixture can be used inside or outdoors.

MICROWAVE PLAY DOUGH

You will need:

- 250 g flour
- 300 g salt
- 2 tsp cream of tartar
- 500 ml water
- 1 tbsp vegetable oil
- Food colouring for coloured play dough

Place all the ingredients into a bowl and stir. Microwave on 'medium' for three minutes, stir, repeat for three minutes on 'medium', and stir again. Cool and knead the dough. To keep it, wrap it in clingfilm or place in an airtight container.

PRAYER CUBE

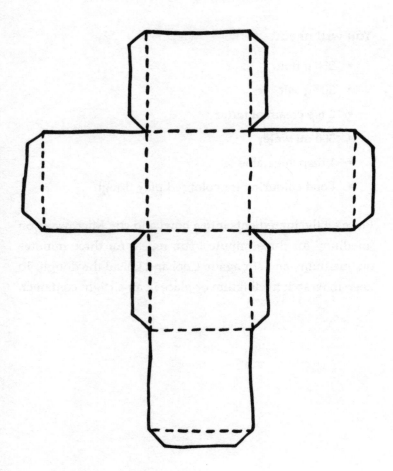

Reproduced with permission from *Messy Prayer* by Jane Leadbetter
(Messy Church, 2015) www.messychurch.org.uk

FLOATING FLOWER

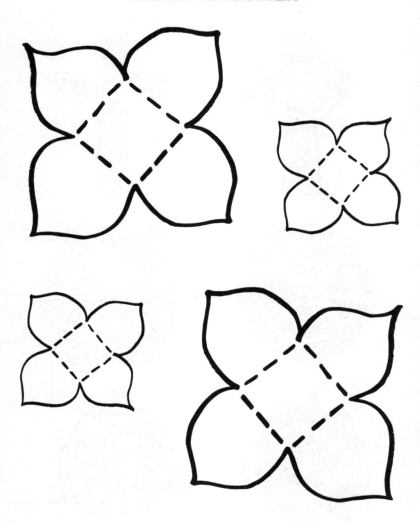

Reproduced with permission from *Messy Prayer* by Jane Leadbetter
(Messy Church, 2015) www.messychurch.org.uk

CELTIC KNOT DESIGNS

Reproduced with permission from *Messy Prayer* by Jane Leadbetter
(Messy Church, 2015) www.messychurch.org.uk

LOVE PRINT

Reproduced with permission from *Messy Prayer* by Jane Leadbetter
(Messy Church, 2015) www.messychurch.org.uk

PEACE SYMBOLS

Reproduced with permission from *Messy Prayer* by Jane Leadbetter
(Messy Church, 2015) www.messychurch.org.uk